Letters to My Broken Mirror

Vaidehi Gajjar

BookLeaf Publishing

Presentation by *BookLeaf Publishing*

Web: www.bookleafpub.com

E-mail: info@bookleafpub.com

ISBN : 9789357699440

First edition 2022

DEDICATION

This book is sincerely dedicated to anyone and everyone struggling to find themselves and realize their place in this world.

The world is too often cruel and unforgiving, with little room to find a space where we are nurtured and loved.

If nowhere else, I dedicate this space to you, reader. Here, you are nurtured and loved.

Finally, to the monkey in my life that consistently teaches me to keep swinging, thank you so much for all the joy and compassion you have brought to me.

ACKNOWLEDGEMENT

I would like to acknowledge the immense appreciation I have for the individuals that have carried me through this life, especially in my darkest times.

This book would not have been a reality for me without the opportunities I have received from mentors that became family, Gerry Dawson, Yvette Santana, Cheyenne Tyler Jacobs, in addition to so many more.

This book, I hope, will serve as a reminder that while there is togetherness in loneliness there is togetherness in healing.

I sincerely hope you find healing from these words, whether it is for your younger self, current self, or future self. May your reflection be seen in the broken pieces of this mirror.

PREFACE

I once heard that while we all may not be in the same boat, we are in the same ocean.

This book aims to capture that very sentiment.

My young mind often struggled with isolation, never finding a true place to belong. Because of this, I worked to create my own identity and worth. This identity and worth was built on the foundation of a very difficult realization:

In order to find yourself, you will lose so much of who and what you thought yourself to be.

p{r}etty minds

I looked in the mirror

And a girl looked back at me

She had my face

She moved when I moved

But she wasn't me

This mirror was a mirror given to me by society

The society that told me my dark skin was ugly

The society that told me to stop being so moody
and
sad

This was the society that told me narrow face

My less than almond-shaped eyes weren't good
enough

And I accepted it

Thinking I was never beautiful

Now I know I've always been my own kind of
beautiful

Blessed with a strong tongue and an even
stronger
mind

So tell me again, society

How ugly I am

Beauty, after all, is in the eye of the beholder

So behold this mind

Behold this soul

Behold this beauty that you refuse to
acknowledge

~V.G

animal vs. the wild

I peek out of the spaces of my cage.

Curious but anxious.

I see multiple pairs of eyes staring back at me.

But not in a good way.

The look in their eyes is scornful, scared
even…but not
understanding.

I reach a hand out hoping someone will do the
same.

It gets slapped away.

Frustrated and sad.

I crawl back into a corner of my cage.

Blinking back tears, I wonder why they treat me
the way they do.

I'm not what I'm seen as.

I know I'm harder to love.

But I need love

More than they know.

To them, love is a very small thing.

But to me?

It's like water to someone stranded in the desert.

Every little drop I get disappears faster than the previous drop I found.

And so I sit in my cage, just searching for that nonexistent love.

They think I'm an animal.

You may think I'm an animal.

But I'm not.

I can promise you that.

I'm just a human. With a mental illness.

~V.G

silence is my voice

Her silences spoke more than her words ever said.

Maybe that's why no one ever heard her when she actually spoke.

She lived in her own little world of darkness, just hoping…just praying.

That someone would hear the screams for help within her silence.

~V.G

friends wanted

I've often driven by or given money to homeless
people that hold up signs that say things like,
"hungry, food needed" or "no money, work
wanted".

I'm thinking of holding up my own sign
somewhere.

Even though none of the signs I've ever held up
have seemed to have worked. I'm going to hold
up my sign, "friends needed".

I've got a home. I've got material things. But
then

Why is it that still…. I feel so homeless with my
invisible sign?

~V.G

the pieces

Here's one thing you should know about people

Like me

People that have been broken

We ask a lot of questions

The ones we've struggled to find answers to

Because we hope that if we find the answer

Somehow we'll be a little more whole again

Somehow our pieces may come back together

And everyone will love us like they love each
other

~V.G

dusk

They said dark skin is

ugly

And I couldn't help but

wonder

What use is a fair complexion

With a charcoal soul

~V.G

lights out

9

She couldn't keep her own flame of hope
flickering

But even still. She stayed very much alive

She may have been gone for what seemed like
eternities

But her desire for the hope she had lost so long
ago

Burned more and more powerful in the hearts of
those

She gave what little hope she had possessed in
her
small

But ever so fierce soul

~V.G

no place to go

Maybe memories hurt so much

Because they're little shards

Of our hearts and souls

That just won't fit back into their
places

~V.G

good morning?

Everyday…it's a struggle

Everyday…it's a fight

A fight with the voices

A fight with…well me

I opened the blinds inside me

hoping the sunlight would pour in

and it did

but yet all I felt was darkness

I was surrounded by light

but all I felt was darkness.

~V.G

invisible ink

Most days I'm just begging myself to be strong.

Acting like I'm okay when I'm really not.

I'm sure I'm not the only one that does this, yet
when I go into this….
mood, I feel quite lonely.

It doesn't ever necessarily leave my brain, just
shifts to
a less visible place.

No, I don't cry a lot anymore.

I just stare…blankly.

No emotion.
No expression.

No nothing.

It's like I'm writing a book hundreds of pages
long, but with a pen that's got no ink.

I've got so much to say, I put effort into it too, it
just never makes it out and into the open.

It's just left in there…in my head.

The world says I'm crazy, and most likely I am.

But to me, crazy was always just another word
for misunderstood.

Horribly, terribly misunderstood….or maybe
just unknown.

~V.G

trash

I thought it was just my food I was

throwing
away

Turns out I was throwing away my

feelings

too

~V.G

mask off

It was exhausting

Most girls came home and took their

makeup off

But me

I came home and took my smile off

Everyone saw through the masks other girls

wore

But somehow no one was able to see through

mine

~V.G

heart lines

If only

The line between practicality and

emotionality could be erased

I can't help but wonder

If people would be different if

The mind had a heart

And the heart had a mind

~V.G

torn

I covered the bumps and scars that outlined my
face

with makeup and they called it 'beauty'

When I covered the angry slashes that
crisscrossed

my arms, they called it 'insecurity'

If they could call my physical scars beautiful,
why

couldn't my invisible scars be just as pretty as
the rest

of me?

~V.G

freedom

What thoughts her heart was too full to carry

Spilled as tears but were seen as ink

Each stroke, an unsung thought

With this she was free

She was finally free

~V.G

survival

19

"What did you do without me?", they
asked.

And for the first time.

She answered without hesitation.

"I survived."

~V. G

heart prints

Sure, I could hear my heart still
pounding where I left it.

But now I can hear my soul talking,
and my mind smiling.

"I'm okay without you", I decide.

~V.G

the worst type of hide and seek

Does it ever end?

Constantly having to lose yourself

After you find yourself

~V.G

return to sender

More often than not

I am an envelope with no

Permanent 'to'

And no permanent 'from'

Too often returned to a sender

That does not exist

~V.G

porcelain

When you heard her pieces shatter
You simply swept them up
And waited for the remnant dust to disappear

But no matter how many times
You waited

The one you thought was porcelain
Slipped through your fingers like smoke
After a forest fire

To find you time and time
Again

~V.G

the girl who lived

Survival was always a familiar concept
She always knew how to gather what
Happiness she could
Like change for a rainy day

It was living that was foreign
The change she collected
Always got spent on someone else

Yet here she was
In all her fear and beauty

Still standing
Still trying to save her change

~V.G

9 789357 699440